D0604338

NO LONGER
PROPERTY OF PPLD

Riverdance

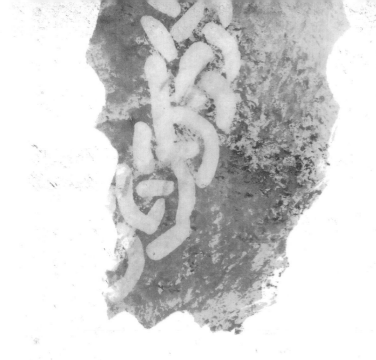

Riverdance

THE STORY

WRITTEN BY
SAM SMYTH

ANDRE
DEUTSCH

FIRST PUBLISHED IN
GREAT BRITAIN IN 1996 BY
ANDRE DEUTSCH
106 GREAT RUSSELLL STREET
LONDON WC1B 3LJ

ALL TEXT © ABHANN
PRODUCTIONS 1996

CIP DATA FOR THIS TITLE
IS AVAILABLE FROM THE
BRITISH LIBRARY

ISBN 0 233 99058 5

BOOK DESIGNED BY
DW DESIGN, LONDON
DESIGN CONSULTANT
ROBERT BALLAGH
PRINTED IN GREAT BRITAIN BY
BUTLER AND TANNER LIMITED.

RIGHT: *Thunderstorm.*
OPPOSITE: *Maria Pagés.*

CONTENTS

ACKNOWLEDGMENTS
6

A HISTORY OF IRISH MUSIC
AND DANCE
8

THE STORY
16

THEMES
80

THE MUSIC
92

THE PRODUCTION
102

THE FUTURE
110

Acknowledgments

The preliminary leg-work for Riverdance: The Book was an enjoyable exercise against daily newspaper deadlines throughout the summer and autumn of 1995 and the spring of 1996 in Dublin, London and New York. The detailed research and final writing was an intense, and occasionally anxious, experience in the dog days of summer 1996, in Dublin. It regularly tried my patience and occasionally sapped a fan's enthusiasm, but my admiration for the artists who created and perform this eclectic and inspired theatrical work has survived undiminished, even enhanced.

I couldn't have done it without the help and encouragement of more people than there is space to name here. Before Riverdance: The Book, Moya Doherty and John McColgan were professional acquaintances; now I consider them friends. They were much more generous and helpful than I expected or could even have hoped they would be, and despite the occasionally adversarial nature of my task, they gave their full cooperation without caveats, or even

Moya Doherty

disagreeable arguments. Bill Whelan made time in the middle of a particularly hectic working schedule on a film score to meet me and talk about his Riverdance experiences with remarkable candour, perception and good humour. The creators of Riverdance: The Show entrusted their reputations – and in some cases personal and confidential documents and information – to me without preconditions or insisting that their views should prevail over mine. I will always be grateful for that. The enormously talented and generous Angela Ryan provided the historical detail on traditional dance and music. Robert Ballagh, already engaged in other commitments, offered me most prescient insight and couldn't have been more generous with anecdotes and information. Mick O'Gorman and Jen Kelly shared their enthusiasm and experiences with style and wit. The urbane Julian Erskine, a pilgrim father of the Riverdance adventure, supplied technical data and gems of information from his encyclopaedic knowledge of the production and its people. A friend for many years, Maurice Cassidy is an honest and

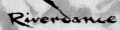

honourable man in a profession not noted for modesty and understatement; he was an invaluable source who dismissed showbiz hyperbole and told the truth, warts and all. I had never met Barry Clayman before, but he couldn't have been more obliging in sharing his wealth of experience. Then there was the team at Abhann Productions, and particularly Joan Egan and Sally O'Neill, who gave me the kind of support which will make going back to real life after Riverdance: The Book all the more difficult. I salute the cast and crew of Riverdance: The Show for their unfailing patience and courtesy; and the inimitable doyen of Irish publicists, Gerry Lundberg, deserves a bouquet. The Editor of the Irish Independent, Vincent Doyle, a rare journalistic combination of success, decency and talent, allowed me the freedom to complete this book. A special thank you to Tim Forrester, the Managing Director of André Deutsch, an early riser who crossed the time zones between Britain and Ireland without suffering culture shock. And my eternal gratitude to the two

Bill Whelan

John McColgan

Faelas, Sarah and Charlotte, who put up with my deadline tantrums with their stoic good humour in the privacy of our home, and brought calm to my life while I took chaos to theirs.

 CHAPTER 1

A HISTORY OF IRISH MUSIC AND DANCE

![Riverdance]

RIVERDANCE: A HISTORY OF IRISH MUSIC AND DANCE

Riverdance is merely a contemporary affirmation of an ancient Irish tradition in which dance and music are celebrated as a metaphor for life. Throughout history Irish men and women have kicked out in time to express an inner joy and stepped in rhythm to consolidate their social circle. No one knows when dancing became a separate and recognised artistic expression, although people probably leapt in time with their whoops when lunch came home on the end of a spear.

Although the origins of Irish music have been recorded by legends, carvings and manuscripts going back nearly a thousand years, the Irish-language word for dance, *damhsa*, first appeared in 1520, a derivation of the English *dance* and French *danse*. The Normans, who invaded Ireland in 1169, are credited with introducing the round dance, or carol, a style of dancing in a circle around a leader. But while the round dances performed in the Pale, the area of direct British influence around Dublin, had polite titles like 'Trotting the Hey' and 'Skipping Gort', beyond the Pale the dances had more explicit titles such as 'Rince Fada Re Racaireacht Ogbhan' (The Long Dance with the Sporting of Young Maidens).

The Fenian Lay, a type of ballad celebrating the incredible feats of the semi-mythological Fionn and his warriors, the Fianna (based on the third century militia under the rule of King Cormac Mac Airt), came to the fore in the twelfth century. The airs to which the ballads were originally set have been lost and Irish schoolchildren now study them as poems. From the time of the Statutes of Kilkenny in 1367, pipers were forbidden to enter the Pale and anyone giving them shelter was guilty of an offence. Irish traditional music and dance also suffered major setbacks under Queen Elizabeth I's rule in the sixteenth century. Although she declared a liking for the Irish jig, her deputies attempted to outlaw Irish bards and musicians. Worried that music and dance could foster Irish nationalism and dissent, the authorities even hanged some

Douglas Hyde (top) and Piper plus Gaelic League Crest (left), both Robert Ballagh designs on Irish £50 note.

Irish manners in 1581, a woodcut from John Derrick's 'Image of Irelande'.

pipers. However, the court of Thomas Dubh, tenth Earl of Ormond, a favourite of Elizabeth who referred to him as her 'black husband', was less austere and noted for its dancing and other entertainments.

The communal nature of Irish country dancing continued through the seventeenth century with the Cake Dance, a competition which awarded the winning couple an edible trophy. In the eighteenth century the solo or step dance emerged, the single most important development in the history of Irish dance, which established the reel, jig and hornpipe as the most popular dances. It was the jig, featuring the rising, grinding and battering steps for men, so familiar in *Riverdance*, which particularly caught the imagination. It was thought to be unladylike for women, who danced the more graceful reel with its rising, sliding steps, shuffle and a promenade movement. The hornpipe, too, was usually only danced by men, although the women of Cork challenged that convention in the late eighteenth century with their spirited dancing of not only the hornpipe, but the traditionally male jig as well. This

first for feminism in dance is still followed by the women dancers in *Riverdance*.

Dance Masters, colourfully affecting the dress and manners of gentlemen, with their knee breeches, silver-buckle shoes and a swallow tail coat, travelled round Ireland from the late eighteenth century teaching the intricate steps. They speeded up the tempo and substituted traditional Irish steps in the quadrilles, or square dances, which were then fashionable in Napoleon's Paris and were brought back to England and Ireland by the Duke of Wellington's

army. Two couples dancing were known as a half-set, a set requiring four couples. Like line dancing two hundred years later, set dancing became a fad, although one that has persisted to the present. There was set dancing at fairs, sporting events and weddings, with the emphasis on camaraderie rather than competition, national celebration rather than nationalist fervour. Dancing at the crossroads became an expression of the natural exuberance of the Irish in this short-lived golden age. And in the late 1930s, Eamon de Valera used 'dancing at the crossroads' as a

metaphor for an idealised Ireland, invoking folk memories of frugal self-sufficiency and innocent entertainment.

The failure of the potato crop between 1845 and 1850 left almost one million dead and forced nearly two million to emigrate. It devastated the country and led to sweeping social changes such as the discouragement of early marriage to ensure that the eldest children stayed at home. Even before the famine, emigrants to North America had taken Irish dancing along the east coast and up into the

Appalachian mountains, where it blended with other folk dances to produce clog and square dancing.

As political resistance to British rule became increasingly militant in the late nineteenth century, Ireland's resolve to hold on to its cultural inheritance stiffened. Douglas Hyde, a Protestant, who was later to become the first President, formed the Gaelic League in 1893 to promote Irish language, music and dance in tandem with the struggle for independence. And the first *ceili* (dance event) took place in London in 1897.

Dancing on the road, 1920's, Glendalough County Wicklow.

Throughout history, civil and religious authority, both foreign and native, have attempted to control the people of Ireland by legislating for music and dancing. In 1930, eight years after independence, in what might have been an inspiration for the xenophobes of the Chinese cultural revolution, the Gaelic League outlawed set dancing as foreign because of its French and Scottish associations, and put the emphasis on solo competition. In Ireland, and in Irish households around the world, the costumes of the young girls taking part in solo dance competitions became stiff and garish, elaborately embroidered with Celtic designs, and the girls' hair was clamped by curling tongs into tightly bound ringlets. There was no historical basis for this new convention, which was a diversion from Irish dancing's traditional spontaneity and sensuality. The Catholic Church lobbied the government to outlaw dances in houses, claiming them to be unhygienic, fire hazards, and frequently organised by the owner of a public house. In 1936 the Dancehall Act required any building used for dancing to be licensed; church halls

became the new entertainment centres.

Although much has been written about the unique style of Irish dance, which insists on keeping the upper body immobile, the acknowledged authority on the traditional music and dancing of Ireland, the late Breandan Breathnach, believed it had more to do with style than with the suppression of sensuality. In his book *Folk Music and Dances of Ireland* (Ossian Publications, Cork), he wrote: 'The good dancer kept the body rigid, moving only from the hips down and with the arms extended straight at the side.' The good dancer 'could dance on eggs without breaking them and hold a pan of water on his head without spilling a drop.'

Seamus O'Se, who runs the O'Shea School of Irish Dancing with his wife Aine, recalls that the World Irish Dancing Championships were established in 1969 and continue to expand and that the first American to be declared a World Champion was a young man from Chicago, Michael Flatley. Vice-President of An Coimisiun le Rinci Gaelacha (The Commission of Irish Dancing), Seamus O'Se says, 'It took *Riverdance*, albeit presented and packaged in a new and exciting format, to awaken the people of Ireland to the rich heritage of our traditional dance. Perhaps, too, it has shown that innovation and imagination need not damage a living tradition but can actually enhance it.'

  Riverdance rescued Irish dancing from the cultural commissars, reclaiming its sensuality with its simple costumes and flowing hair while celebrating its traditions and skills passed through generations. And the resurrection of traditional Irish dancing on an international stage came after Irish music had taken its place as an important strand of contemporary popular culture. The Irish groups U2 and the Cranberries were already major influences in popular music all over the world when *Riverdance* made its debut in the Eurovision Song Contest and went on become a theatrical phenomenon and a metaphor for a new Ireland dancing into the twenty-first century.

OPPOSITE: *Old engraving of a piper, hanged for 'sedition'.*
TOP: *The Blind Piper by Joseph Haverty.*
RIGHT: *Joanna Behan, Leinster Champion 1995-96, in traditional Irish dress.*

CHAPTER 2

THE STORY

RIVERDANCE: THE STORY

Ireland had won the Eurovision Song Contest five times before Moya Doherty was asked to take responsibility for staging the epic three-hour entertainment for television. And while the wins were a transcontinental salute to Irish popular culture, producing the Song Contest for RTE falls somewhere between a patriotic obligation and a professional poisoned chalice. Each triumph was a pyrrhic victory: paying for the most prestigious and lavish spectacle on European television put enormous strains on the national station's modest financial resources and left RTE seriously overdrawn on its talent bank. Just two months after the 1993 final had been transmitted from County Cork and Ireland had won yet again, the Director of Programmes, Liam Miller, rang Moya Doherty and asked if she would take overall charge of the 1994 production from Dublin. While it is one of Europe's smallest national broadcasting companies, RTE provides two television channels for the Republic of Ireland's 3.6 million population and has earned an international reputation for innovation and technical excellence from its Eurovision productions. Getting twenty-five songs into three hours, with satellite trips to each jury voting in the European capitals and side excursions to Africa and Asia, may earn the host station applause from the television industry, but it leaves little room for aesthetics. Over the previous ten years every pyrotechnic trick, audio visual gimmick and electronic gizmo had been spot-welded on to clichéd travelogues plugging tourism in each participating country. And the resulting mishmash of styles had turned the Song Contest into a televisual celebration of Euro kitsch, making the annual search for fresh talent to concoct another permutation of retina-threatening dazzle more and more difficult.

Although she had experience in light entertainment, Moya Doherty's reputation as a serious programme maker had been secured by a sensitive, controversial and award-winning film, *The Silent Scream*, about incest and child abuse in a Dublin

> *The sun is our lord and father,*
> *Bright face at the gate of dawn,*
> *Comfort of the home, cattle and crop,*
> *Lord of the morning, lord of the day.*
>
> REEL AROUND THE SUN – ACT I SCENE I

Jean Butler and Colin Dunne with the Riverdance Troupe.

LEFT: *Jean Butler and Colin Dunne.*

ABOVE: *Joanne Doyle.*

Breandán de Gallaí and male dancers from the Riverdance Troupe.

family. In the summer of 1992, when RTE put on their bi-annual eight-hour fund-raising telethon for charity, they asked Moya Doherty to organise it. Before that she had anchored RTE's television coverage of the 1984 Olympics from Los Angeles, then worked for four years as a reporter/presenter with TV-AM in London. She came home to Ireland in 1989. Living in Howth, a beautiful seaside village ten miles from Dublin, with her husband John McColgan, a television director, she decided to take a two-year break from television and spend more time with their two sons, then aged five and three. She had already turned down a couple of offers from RTE before the Director of Programmes called her in July with the offer of producing the Eurovision Song Contest marathon. 'You really have one full hour to make an impression, and apart from the visual look

> *Dawn, and the*
> *ships are leaving,*
> *A lover's grief is*
> *lifting on the tide,*
> *And hearts too*
> *young for sorrow,*
> *Torn asunder,*
> *The cruel ocean's deep,*
> *and dark, and wide.*
>
> PARTING – ACT II SCENE I

of it there was time to say something, to make a statement, if the programme could actually be produced as opposed to being just a vehicle for songs. I had said I wanted time out and I wasn't really keen on it. But I told Liam I would think about it over the weekend,' recalls Doherty. Never regarded by her peers as particularly ambitious, she talked it over with her husband, who was now managing director of Tyrone Productions, an independent television production company. On Monday she accepted the position of Executive Producer, and began work on the programme in September 1993.

Curiously, it was the interval showpiece rather than the actual Song Contest that intrigued Moya Doherty. 'I think the click was a chorus line and I went straight away and wrote a document for Liam Miller.' The memorandum ignored the two hours fifty-five minutes of the contest and results and concentrated on the five-minute space between the last song and the first vote from a jury. Doherty wrote: 'Essentially it would be a five-minute commissioned work from a contemporary Irish composer. A percussive piece which would give us an opportunity to showcase top Irish musicians, dancers, performers and singers. The core of the number would be a vibrant, sexy, contemporary Irish tap dance routine starring Jean Butler, first generation

Irish American living in Birmingham, and Michael Flatley, first generation Irish American residing in Los Angeles.' It came with a warning: 'This would not be a "back to our roots" routine, rather the opposite.' Under a sub-heading, 'The Shape of the Piece', she continued: 'We begin with a lonely band of musicians on a big empty stage, enter the pageantry up the centre of the auditorium, a hundred marching Bodhran players ... all this with a chorus of Irish voices... From a point of darkness ... enter row upon row of hard-shoe Irish dancers and they pound their way downstage towards audience and camera... They stream apart to the dramatic entrance of the star dancers who perform their energetic routine. Gradually the tempo increases, bringing all the ingredients together in an exhilarating climax.'

TOP AND BOTTOM: *Michael Flatley and Jean Butler.*
OPPOSITE: *American Wake.*

Riverdance

It was composer Bill Whelan who came up with the title *Riverdance*.

And so *Riverdance* began in five paragraphs on a single sheet of paper.

Earlier that year, in June, John McColgan, a former Controller of Programmes at Britain's TV-AM and Head of Entertainment at RTE, had produced 'Mayo 5000: The Celebration Concert', honouring the rugged county in the far west of Ireland. Two Irish American dancers, Jean Butler from Long Island and Michael Flatley from Chicago, both with family links to Mayo, performed individually, although the concert was principally a vehicle for contemporary Irish composer Bill Whelan's 'The Spirit of Mayo', featuring an 85-piece orchestra, a choir of 200 singers and a battalion of drummers. But it was the dancers who caught Moya Doherty's eye:

LEFT: *Jean Butler, Colin Dunne and the Riverdance Troupe.*
BELOW: *President Mary Robinson meeting members of the Riverdance Troupe.*

'When I saw Michael I thought, Wow. You could see bits of flamenco, bits of tap, bits of Irish, and then I saw Jean, who was dancing with Colin Dunne at the time. She was beautiful and a very striking dancer. She wore a simple black short skirt and her hair was very plain, everything about her was uncluttered and uncomplicated.' Moya Doherty rang Bill Whelan. 'The first meeting was in Fitzer's restaurant in Baggot Street in Dublin. We sat at a table by the window,' recalls Whelan. 'I worked ten and twelve hour days on it over the next couple of months. The first draft was completed in early December. It was based on the life of a river: quiet at source, it would interact with the land, feeding it and nourishing it, and rush out to the sea at the estuary. There was a quiet opening choral piece and a large finale - that was the germ of the idea. The lyrics were the last to be added.' Moya Doherty contacted Michael Flatley at his home in Beverly Hills and booked him for the Eurovision Song Contest the following April. It took several days to track down Jean Butler, who was touring in Japan with the Chieftains, and she also agreed to appear in the programme.

ANÚNA, a Dublin-based singing group of seven men and seven women, had been part of Bill Whelan's Spirit of Mayo Suite, and they had sung on recording sessions with Elvis Costello, Sting, Sinead

O'Connor and Maire Brennan of Clannad. Their leader, Michael McGlynn, had taken some long forgotten musical works of the ancient Celts and recreated them as haunting and intricate choral pieces. Whelan considered them essential for his purpose. Then he booked a team of four drummers to add a primeval base to his complex score. An old friend of Moya Doherty choreographer Mavis Ascott, was contracted and she arranged a work schedule with Bill Whelan. Tapes of Bill Whelan's music were couriered to Michael Flatley in California and Jean Butler in England, where she was doing a course in theatre studies at Birmingham University. And the Executive Producer of Eurovision negotiated an unheard-of luxury from RTE: flying in Michael Flatley from the United States and Jean Butler from England for a week of meetings in January. Auditions were hurriedly arranged to allow Mavis Ascott and Michael Flatley to see the troupe of twenty-four Irish dancers with whom they would be working; it surprised no one when eighteen of them came from the O'Shea school in Dublin. Costumes were air-freighted to Jean Butler and Michael Flatley and adjustments were discussed on the telephone. Three weeks before the Eurovision Song Contest, both dancers flew into Dublin to begin rehearsals.

Although Bill Whelan and Moya Doherty

Oscail an Doras (open the door).

had worked out the piece very clearly on paper – 'Entrances and exits; male dancer, female dancer; the build ups; both principals gone, both come back; joined by some dancers, then more' – it needed staging and professional choreography. Michael Flatley worked on the Irish dance steps for the chorus and his own routines while Jean Butler concentrated on her own steps. 'It was all broken up,' recalls Moya Doherty. 'It was a question of how they would put it back together. Meanwhile I was absorbed in delivering the Eurovision programme and there were delegates and hundreds of people arriving from all over the world, but I just knew it was great. I was unhappy with just a couple of things, and one of them was the on-stage relationship between Jean and Michael. They ended up hugging each other or she ended up sitting on his knee. I said, "No... the sexual chemistry has to be distant..."' Although she was a very experienced choreographer, Mavis Ascott, who was born in East London, had no particular expertise in Irish dancing, but she pulled it all together. Traditionally in Irish dancing the arms are held tightly into the sides and the back is ramrod stiff, permitting body movements only from the waist down: presumably this exhibition of Puritanism at play was part conceived as an exercise in anti-eroticism. Although *Riverdance* tapped into the genre's subliminal sexuality, its presentation was still

coy, and the women's costumes would be shorter than regulation competition dresses, this was for practical reasons, to permit freedom of movement. From the first dress rehearsals and previews there were standing ovations, and the planned five-minute interval had been extended to seven. 'I was so busy, I thought, "that piece of the show is going to work anyway,"' says Moya Doherty. 'On 30 April, the night the Eurovision programme was transmitted, I was waiting for all the satellite links from all the juries to come in. The voting came immediately after the *Riverdance* interval. I had my eye on the monitor but I was talking to Sarajevo when RTE's head of sound, Charlie Byrne, said, "They're up." I said, "Who's up?" and he said, "The audience are up on their feet."'

It was seven minutes that shattered the hermetically sealed world of television, seizing the attention and igniting the imagination of 300 million viewers. Something happened. It was one of those rare moments when indifference was suspended and it left an indelible imprint on the memory of anyone who experienced it. Bill Whelan's music soared, uplifting Michael Flatley and inspiring Jean Butler, while the

chorus line of hard shoes beat out the Irish rhythm of life and ANÚNA's ethereal voices transported the television audience to the Point in Dublin. Meanwhile, in the theatre, the 3,000 people dressed up in evening wear leapt out of their seats when its thundering climax brought the seven-minute spectacle to an end. Ireland's usually reserved President Mary Robinson was one of the first on her feet. The delegations from twenty-five countries sat mesmerised with the Irish dignitaries during the performance and they all leapt up spontaneously when it finished. 'It wasn't a cheer, but a roar, a primeval roar,' said John McColgan. 'People were crying.' *Riverdance*: The Phenomenon was born on 30 April 1994, in a Dublin theatre with 3,000 people in attendance, before a television audience of 300 million. And Ireland's entry, 'Rock n Roll Kids', won the Eurovision Song Contest.

A week later, the *Riverdance* single had entered the Irish Top Ten at Number One. It stayed at the top for eighteen weeks, and later reached Number

Thunder and lightening batter the rocks, The winds howl and great storms Break on the forest, scatter the herds like grain.

THUNDERSTORM – ACT I SCENE V

Nine in the British record charts. It went on sale only the day before the Eurovision programme. Whelan couldn't convince any record company of its commercial potential and, with the managing director of his music publishing company, Barbara Galavan, he eventually persuaded an insurance company, Church and General, to pay for the recording.

Like everyone involved, Moya Doherty was totally exhausted after the Eurovision Song Contest. 'I had no real experience of the hard commercial world, so I wasn't thinking of its financial potential. In fact that is one of the really good things about *Riverdance*: it grew out of public service broadcasting, out of a desire to do something positive.' But John McColgan spotted its creative and commercial possibilities and urged his wife to do a full theatrical production. Then Liam Miller asked if she would develop *Riverdance* as an hour-long Christmas special for RTE. The television industry's admiration of the Eurovision spectacle spread by word of mouth, it received very positive reviews in the international press, the record

ABOVE: *Eurovision performance, Dublin 1994.*

OPPOSITE: *Masks for the Prince's Trust, 1996, handpainted by Robert Ballagh.*

36 | THE STORY

was Number One in the Irish charts and rising in the British Top Ten. Moya Doherty believed a one-off Christmas special for television would squander the potential of a concept about which she had grown fiercely protective. As the demand for a video grew in Ireland, the Rwandan tragedy was dominating television news bulletins and it was agreed to release the video with the entire proceeds donated to charities working with the victims in central Africa. It was the fastest selling video in Irish history and raised nearly £300,000 for relief in Rwanda. Inadvertently, the reaction to the video was an instructive piece of market research: it was a must at students' parties - and four-year-olds were playing it over and over like a Disney classic; the feedback suggested that *Riverdance* appealed to all age groups. John McColgan said that if people were forking out £10 for a seven minute video, they would pay the market price to watch a two hour stage show. Bill Whelan was keen to develop the project and arranged for his partner in a publishing company, Paul McGuinness, manager of the rock band U2, to meet Moya and John. 'I said what we need is for John, Bill and myself to go away to do some research and decide what this is,' says Moya Doherty. RTE matched the £10,000 development money put up by Paul McGuinness.

A concept for a two-hour show was at the

top of the agenda, and a loose story outline was put together by Whelan and Doherty with McColgan. But there was another factor that couldn't be ignored. They all knew that they would be held accountable if the integrity of their production did not match up to the rigorous standards demanded by the Praetorian Guard of Ireland's cultural heritage. They represented the first generation since the Republic of Ireland's independence to experience material prosperity and were conscious of suspicions that they might sell out their responsibility to a heritage passed down through centuries. In a country where cultural identity was repressed for hundreds of years and freedom was in living memory paid for in blood and tears, no one dare play fast and loose with its unique artistic expressions of national pride.

'We had an idea for a great opening number and a show-stopping finish,' says Moya Doherty, 'but there was a structure in the middle to be filled in.' John McColgan was convinced there was a demand for a *Riverdance* stage show, but knew that realising it would be difficult. Obviously the dancing would be built round Jean Butler, Michael Flatley and the team of traditional dancers who had been at the heart of the television piece. But for a two-hour show they needed something else - a shared experience told through dance.

'The problem was that Moya and Bill found that most folk dancing could stun a sheep at twenty paces,' says John McColgan. Bill Whelan and Moya Doherty, with Michael Flatley, travelled across Europe seeking talent and inspiration. Their first stop was in the cultural capital of Andalucia, Seville, to meet flamenco dancer Maria Pagés, one of the of most celebrated classical dancers in Spain, with whom Bill Whelan had worked for the European premiere of *The Seville Suite*, an orchestral work he was commissioned to write for Expo '92. Both Doherty and Whelan were convinced that Flatley and Pages would be a formidable combination. Then they went to Hungary, and struck gold again: Nikola Parov, a musician who two years earlier had introduced Bill Whelan to the complex rhythms of eastern Europe; but they didn't find any suitable dancers in Budapest. Russian dancers, preferably acrobatic Cossacks, titillated the imaginations of Doherty and McColgan but nothing came of their enquiry to the Russian embassy in Dublin. The team's offices on the quays of the river Liffey in Dublin were gradually becoming submerged under boxes of video-tapes of folk dancers from all over the world. In despair, Moya Doherty had stopped looking at them. Then one morning a tape arrived on John McColgan's desk. It was stunning, an artful marriage of folk and classical dance performed with

breathtaking acrobatic skill. The three-men, three-women troupe, the Moscow Folk Ballet Company, had originally came together at the respected Moiseyev Dance Company in Moscow. It was just what the composer, producer and director had in mind.

Bill Whelan believed gospel music should be an integral part of *Riverdance's* journey and went to see James Bignon and the Deliverance Ensemble, a twelve-piece choir, in Atlanta, Georgia. He was bowled over with what he saw and heard, offered them a contract, and they agreed to come to Dublin. The second half of the show needed other dancers who would be strikingly different and provide a contrast to the Irish company. Three streetwise dudes, dazzling African American tap dancers, Marcel Peneux, Leon Hazelwood and Jelly Germaine, were taken on to do a routine with Michael Flatley, himself at one time listed in the *Guinness Book of Records* as the world's fastest tap dancer.

It would be impossible to over-emphasise the importance of Bill Whelan's contribution, although it often gets overlooked in such a spectacularly visual show. His music is the vehicle that takes *Riverdance* through its two-hour journey; it builds the emotional peaks and provides the intricate rhythms from which the dancing takes off. Integrating the international music and dance with the Irish traditional roots of *Riverdance: The Show* was a complex operation. The show is primarily a celebration of Irish traditional music and dance, but the excursions into the music and dance of other traditions don't induce culture shock. Whelan decided that the singing group ANÚNA was the base on which he would build the vocal score, although a guest singer, Aine Ui Cheallaigh, sang the song that has proved to be *Riverdance's* most enduringly popular; 'Lift the Wings'. But Whelan believed the band was the musical heart of *Riverdance*, that the show would stand or fall on the performances of the musicians as much as those of the dancers. He saw them as an integral part of the show and lifted them out of the orchestra pit and onto the stage. Those who were not successful recording artists in their own right were among the most sought after session musicians. Nor did Whelan limit himself to Irish-based musicians: Nikola Parov, his old friend and colleague from an

earlier album, 'East Winds', was brought in from Budapest to play gadulka, kaval and gaida for the East European rhythms; flamenco guitarist Rafael Riquenti accompanied Maria Pages. The musical director, David Hayes, played keyboards, Maire Breathnach was on fiddle, Mairtin O'Connor played accordion. Davy Spillane alternated between Uilleann pipes and low whistles, Kenneth Edge doubled on soprano and alto saxophones, Desi Reynolds played drums and percussion while Noel Eccles busied himself on a whole suite of percussion instruments. Des Moore showed off his skills on several guitars, Eoghan O'Neill played bass guitar, and Tommy Hayes beat the Bodhran when he wasn't banging the Dunbeg or alternating between spoons and bones. It was the most

expensive theatre band ever to play in Ireland or Great Britain. 'The band are a group of my friends and associates and we allowed them to become part of the presentation, interacting with the cast and integrated in the show. They were expensive, but John and Moya have never been slow to pay for quality,' says Bill Whelan.

The original set at the Point in Dublin, designed by Mary Morrow of RTE, with Andrew Leonard's artful lighting, transformed the huge auditorium into an intimate theatre while colouring the mood and highlighting the drama on stage. Later, Moya Doherty called on painter Robert Ballagh to design the London and touring production. Chris Slingsby was given the task of projecting Ballagh's original oil-on-canvas paintings onto the stage. Dublin-based lighting designer Rupert Murray, who had just finished working on Jonathan Miller's production of Goldsmith's *She Stoops to Conquer*, was called in to light the show. Costume designer Jen Kelly from Derry worked for RAI television in Italy and the Fox network in Los Angeles before he got the call to design the costumes for *Riverdance*. London-born Michael O'Gorman, who had worked on such events as the RTE Proms and the gala 250th anniversary performance of Handel's *Messiah* in Dublin, was drafted in to design the sound.

The Gaiety, an elegant traditional theatre in the heart of Dublin, was an obvious venue but it wasn't big enough for *Riverdance: The Show*. 'We figured that if we mounted it on a certain scale, with the kind of set we had in mind and an international cast of eighty, it would transcend an Irish event. And we had budgeted the show at £1.3 million,' says John McColgan. The vast 3,500-seater Point, a multi-purpose entertainment centre near Dublin's docklands, was provisionally booked for the second week in February 1995. RTE Enterprises came up with £200,000 and then Paul McGuinness's £50,000 was matched by another Dublin-based promoter, Maurice Cassidy, who in turn brought in a friend, Tommy Higgins, who stumped up another £50,000. Moya Doherty persuaded a bank and Harry Crosbie, a Dublin property developer who had a share in the Point, to come up with £50,000 between them. Doherty's company with John McColgan, Abhann Productions, was co-ordinating all the pre-production work. And Doherty was anxious: 'The balance of the money, £800,000, was the risk that John and I had to take. And there was a moment, at eleven o'clock one night after a particularly tense day, when we were driving down the docks on our way home, and I said, "John, I wouldn't even bet on a horse, I'm so cautious. What about our children? What about the

house?" He looked at me and said, "Moya, this is going to work." And I said, "Okay, that's it."' They needed to sell 40 per cent of the available 3,500 tickets for each of the twenty-one performances to cover their own risk. And that didn't pay the bills: the break-even point was around 70 per cent. But just when their nerves were dangerously jangling, another sprinkling of *Riverdance*'s pixie dust brought it back to prime time television audiences in Britain: the

OPPOSITE: *Michael Flatley and Jean Butler..*

RIGHT: *HRH Prince Charles meeting Michael Flatley and Jean Butler.*

company was asked to perform the original seven minute version at the Royal Variety Show in the presence of HRH Prince Charles.

Meanwhile, back at the office, the management of the Point was pushing for their booking to be confirmed. Mavis Ascott was already committed to direct her own Christmas show, and Michael Flatley took over as choreographer. While the rest of the cast, including thirty World Champion Irish dancers, rehearsed in Dublin, Maria Pages put her routines together in Seville; the gospel choir worked on their pieces in Atlanta; and the Moiseyev troupe put their steps to Bill Whelan's music played on a cassette in their rehearsal room in Moscow. After the most anxious three months of their lives, everyone relaxed following a guest appearance on RTE's 'Late Late Show'. Michael Flatley and six of the male dancers performed one of the new numbers, 'Distant Thunder', and he and Jean Butler were interviewed. As the tickets went on sale, Moya Doherty telephoned the presenter Gay Byrne, an old

I was the land and the land was me. Tall and straight I walk in the world But bell and cross banished my comfort.

SHIVNA – ACTI SCENE VI

friend and Ireland's most popular talk show host. As they chatted casually, she confided: 'Gay, my neck is on the line, I really am at financial risk.' On his programme, Gay Byrne said a pair of tickets would make an imaginative gift. This did the trick, and it seemed that everybody in Ireland, and their mother, got a present of *Riverdance* tickets for Christmas 1994. By that time Julian Erskine had been brought in as Executive Manager by the Dublin promoter Maurice Cassidy, but he wore another hat as Technical Co-ordinator for Abhann productions. 'The box office opened to record-breaking ticket sales and I remember checking with the Ticket Shop in Dublin just before Christmas and ringing Moya and telling her the sales had topped £1 million. The next phone call to Moya was just after Christmas when we passed the break-even figure of £1.3 million.' Maurice Cassidy came up with the tactic of putting out tickets for only twenty-one performances and then adding another two weeks. The entire five-week run had sold before the show opened.

ABOVE: *Marcel Peneux, Leon Hazelwood and Jelly Germaine.*

Some Dublin critics had expressed concerns that the integrity of Irish traditional arts, passed on to successive generations since medieval times, would be vulgarised by the show. They needn't have worried: the opening, on 9 February 1995, was universally acclaimed as a popular and artistic triumph. And while there was just one standing ovation, it lasted nearly thirty minutes; in fact few of the audience bothered to sit down again and simply made their way out of the Point. Several critics awarded *Riverdance: The Show* the accolade of placing it alongside Brian Friel's modern masterpiece for the theatre, *Dancing at Lughnasa*. It won the approval of

TOP: *The Deliverance Ensemble from Atlanta, Georgia.*
ABOVE: *Moscow Folk Ballet Company.*

the most conservative cultural organisations and the praise of both contemporary and traditional artists.

The Apostolic Nuncio saw the show, as did the Taoiseach, the United States Ambassador, Jean Kennedy Smith, the British Ambassador, David Blatherwick, and most of the diplomatic corps in Dublin; in fact anyone who was, or considered themselves to be, important in Ireland on 9 February 1995. Beyond the theatre, a great swell of national pride overflowed from *Riverdance: The Show* into the consciousness of ordinary Irish people who never let culture get in the way of having a good time. It was

just music, singing and dancing, the same basic ingredients that can make a success of any Irish house party, except that at the Point they were performed with style and gusto by some of the country's finest artists and their international guests. It was probably the first time that many Irish people heard the music and dancing with which they grew up and took for granted, presented and performed with at least as much sophistication and excitement as anything from Broadway or the West End. And it was the sheer power of the set pieces, where Whelan's music fused with Flatley's brilliantly creative choreography, closing the first and second acts which were the highlights of the evening. The integration of Russian, Spanish and African American culture drew unanimous applause from the Irish audience – and their reaction confirmed to its producer and investors that *Riverdance: The Show* had wings that would take it beyond Ireland.

British impresario Barry Clayman was in Dublin with a party of friends from London for the second night. He has promoted evenings with Frank Sinatra, the Kirov Ballet and Barbra Streisand and is not easily impressed. 'As a promoter it is not my job to fall in love with shows and artists, but I absolutely loved it. I can't remember when I was so moved in a theatre. I can explain anything about show business, it's my job. But I gave up trying to explain *Riverdance*.'

Jean Butler and Colin Dunne.

Clayman was introduced to Maurice Cassidy backstage and a partnership was born. Good news travels nearly as fast as hot gossip in show business and Maurice Cassidy advised that they waste no time moving the show to London. Moya Doherty, John McColgan and Maurice Cassidy met Barry Clayman in London and

he showed them the three most likely venues: the Royal Albert Hall, Wembley Arena and the rundown Apollo theatre in Hammersmith. There was an overpowering smell of disinfectant in the Apollo and the theatre badly needed decoration. But the management promised to spend £1 million

refurbishing the 3,500 seater and offered a good deal on the rent. Since neither the Royal Albert Hall nor Wembley Arena would be available for an extended run, they decided on Hammersmith. If they needed any further omens for success, another came on 7 April when the Irish video release of *Riverdance: The Show* went straight to Number One in the best-seller charts. Then, as the company prepared to cross the Irish sea, Prince Charles gave the London ticket sales a boost when he personally invited the cast to perform at the Royal Gala to celebrate VE Day at the London Coliseum, which was seen by some 20 million television viewers. There were some changes made for the London production: Aine Ui Cheallaigh, who sang the haunting 'Lift the Wings', dropped out and ANÚNA performed it as a duet; the band's own guitarist, Des Moore, took over from Maria Pagés's flamenco guitarist Rafael Riqueni when he had to return to Spain. And there was a lot of excitement when Bill Whelan brought Eileen Ivers, a seven times All Ireland Fiddle Champion, born of Irish parents in the Bronx, New York, to replace Maire Breatnach.

It was speculated that *Riverdance: The Show* moved to Hammersmith because of the large Irish population living in the west London borough. The truth was less fanciful: with a payroll of more than a hundred, no West End theatre was big enough and

ANÚNA.

Riverdance, the finale.

every one of the Labatt Apollo's 3,200 seats (300 had to be removed to accommodate the band) was needed to cover the £1.5 million investment. And there was another concern which people didn't like to talk about: would Londoners pay a top ticket price of £27.50 to see an Irish show after twenty-six years of the Northern Ireland troubles and their reverberations in the British capital? They got their answer when the box office opened: *Riverdance: The Show* was the hottest ticket in town. It had found its time and place. A paramilitary cease-fire in Northern Ireland had allowed optimism to blossom, but the cessation of hostilities alone couldn't explain the show's appeal. For some reason Ireland and all things Irish were

fashionable. And it wasn't the cheap scent of nostalgia, or a begorra look at the quaintness of it all. The stage Irishism that had cast its men as amiable or pugilistic drunks, and its women as retiring or fiery redheads in a shawl, was anathema to Ireland in the mid-1990s. With more than 50 per cent of its population under 25 years old, the Irish nation was no longer touching its forelock or looking over its shoulder as it moved towards the twenty-first century. U2 had featured on the cover of *Time* magazine as 'The Hottest Ticket in Rock'; Irish films were among the hottest tickets in cinema; Dublin weekends were the hottest tickets in European tourism; the Irish soccer team, with an English manager, had distinguished itself in the World Cup.

In their parents' lifetime, 'No Irish' signs on the windows of lodging houses had been socially respectable in the same foreign capitals where their articulate, well educated emigrant children were now in demand as executives and administrators in financial services companies and arts centres. And they brought more than sophistication with them: the lap top generation had packed their hand-me-down culture along with their cut-down Levi's. This remarkable new tolerance grew out of a revival of traditional Irish music which had coincided with the rise and rise of rock 'n roll in the 1960s, when bearded folkies sat comfortably alongside Beatles fans in the dingy basement clubs of Dublin. And while the old and new played happily together at home for twenty years, they also exported the phenomenon overseas: The Chieftains packed the major concert halls of the world, while U2 filled stadiums.

The day before it opened in London, *Riverdance: The Show* was released as a video and entered the British best seller lists at Number Two, moved to the top slot the following week and

Whole generations lift now to depart. The land has failed us, the dark soldiers appear against us. In dance and song we gift and mourn our children. They carry us over the ocean in dance and song.

AMERICAN WAKE – ACT II SCENE I

alternated between the first and second positions for the next seven months. Still, some pundits wondered if the show's uncompromising Irishness would be comprehensible to a non-Irish audience in the theatre? The previews drew capacity houses and enthusiastic reviews from the British critics; the opening, on 6 June 1995, challenged the perception in Ireland that first-night audiences in London were irredeemably inhibited. There were five standing ovations.

Maybe half of the opening-night audience was Irish, but many of the others wanted to be: it was an unnerving, if flattering, experience for many of the bemused Irish in the Labatt Apollo. *Riverdance: The Show* proved to be an equal opportunity theatrical experience, taking its audience, regardless of nationality, on a helter-skelter ride through their emotions. Davy Spillane's lament on the Uilleann pipes dipped the mood to reflective melancholy; spines tingled spontaneously when ANÚNA's 'Lift the Wings' set the tone for the second act; the clack of seventy pairs of hard shoes on resonant wood raised the hairs on the back of necks, then made some of the audience laugh out loud as the finale thundered to its exhilarating climax. Maria Pagés's whirling flamenco married sensuality to classical dance; the dignity of the African American gospel singers in gowns gave an uncomfortable reminder of how some emigrants left their homelands for America in chains; the breathtaking acrobatics, turbo-charged energy and rigid discipline of the

Moscow Folk Ballet Company brought the audience to its feet; and the slick routines of tap dancers Marcel Peneux, Leon Hazelwood and Jelly Germaine were an amusing urban diversion from the rural Irish heartland which is the source of *Riverdance*.

At times, the traditional jigs, reels and hornpipes of Ireland jarred awkwardly alongside the dances and songs of the show's international guests. The production wasn't a smooth purée blended from all of its component parts, but it was all the richer for its diversity. And the notion of an international brotherhood and sisterhood of dance was no less honourable an aspiration for its naivety. Whelan's original score was crafted so skilfully that audiences were convinced all the tunes and songs were traditional classics. Yet Michael Flatley's and Jean Butler's individual performances, and the sheer spectacle of a battalion of disciplined and drilled Irish traditional dancers, were what made *Riverdance* different from anything before it. The dancers' youthful energy artfully concealed

Jean Butler, Bill Whelan, Denise Whelan, Moya Doherty; Plaza Hotel, New York, after first Radio City performance.

The entire Riverdance Company, St. Patrick's Day,
Radio City, New York.

57 | THE STORY

PREVIOUS SPREAD: American Wake (inset) Jean Butler and Colin Dunne.

their dedicated professionalism, and it took long hours of rehearsal and practice to make the chorus appear like amateurs in a competition. It was Michael Flatley's obsessional drive for perfection in rehearsal, both for himself and the other dancers, that turned the unabashed enthusiasm and raw energy of last year's amateurs into this year's polished professionals.

There lies a significant part of the *Riverdance* secret: no one connected with *Riverdance: The Show* had ever done anything like it before. Although Moya Doherty, the producer, had wanted to work in the theatre since her childhood, her career had taken her into television. Like most of the others in the company, she was new to the economic and practical problems of staging a theatrical show. It was like the let's-put-on-a-show plot of an old MGM musical, where starry-eyed amateurs take on the veteran professionals and have a hit against all the odds. The London opening was a triumph of energy and optimism over theatrical experience, and every seat was sold for the four-week run. It was the hit show in the early summer of 1995 in London,

Out of the night we come, out of the sea. On a new shore, lights blaze in the dawn.

THE HARBOUR OF THE NEW WORLD – ACT II SCENE II

with harassed hotel receptionists having to deal with touts demanding more than double the face value for tickets. The critics ladled praise on the company, picking up on the vitality of the performers and the energy and sensitivity of the music. And its social cachet was confirmed when *Riverdance: The Show* was invited to perform at a charity gala evening, titled 'Ninety Years of Dance and Music', in the presence of Her Majesty Queen Elizabeth II and HRH Princess Margaret. But real life occasionally intruded on the gee-whiz world of the showbiz rookies, especially for many of the young Irish dancers who had never stayed away from home before without their parents. One young dancer was in tears and couldn't explain it: there she was, 18 years old, living out a fantasy on a London stage in a hit show and earning more money than she had ever dreamed of, yet she was weeping uncontrollably. She was homesick. There were queues at the pay phones backstage every night, although the charges were reversed on most of the calls home. The performers shared anxieties and

New York Gala Première

RADIO CITY MUSIC HALL, MARCH 14TH 1996

applause, ambitions and insecurities, exaggerated in proportion to their distance from home, a bedrock from which an almost indestructible camaraderie developed. Outsiders noticed it backstage, but the cast socialised together too. One member of the company was appointed as a sort of social secretary, organising tickets to see other shows; there were trips to Oxford, Alton Towers, amusement parks, karaoke nights and pub quizzes. There was even a *Riverdance* 'Trivial Pursuit' game, with questions like: how many pairs of shoes are shined before each show? Answer: 85. Maximum number of dancers on stage at any one time? 70. Bottles of mineral water consumed by the cast each week? 1,000. Number of lights of stage? 450.

Injuries took their toll too, and at any time during a run two or three of the cast would be resting, their places taken by stand-ins. The dancers' leg joints took a shocking pounding every night and

physiotherapists were kept damaged muscles and trea And there were stories cr newspapers about strains and Jean Butler. They we but people who had seen remarked that there appe between them at the Ap at the Point three months befo

Although they had before rehearsals began in Dub the Point in July 1995, there w of the young dancers who had practically non-stop since Febr recalled that three days before t dancers slept in the corridors o dress rehearsal in the afternoon night. 'I suggested they use the room,' she said. Designer Robe down on many of the architect set, leaving the stage totally fre with projected slides of his fort paintings to achieve the moods the show opened on a Saturday its social status as a vehicle for t Irish at home or away. The gal charity, was a glittering affair w

jostling with the rich and famous children of the Diaspora. Film director Neil Jordan took a night off from filming his Michael Collins epic and arrived with actors Aidan Quinn and Stephen Rea. Maureen O'Hara, who had been the role model for fiery redheaded Irish womanhood two generations earlier in the first major Hollywood film set in Ireland, *The Quiet Man*, gave her seal of approval. It was an Irish audience's first opportunity to see a new creation for the opening of the second act, 'American Wake'. This is one of the most poignant scenes in *Riverdance*, telling the story of how poverty and famine drove millions of Irish from their homeland to emigrate to the United States in the mid-nineteenth century. An 'American Wake' was the parting of loved ones from their families, knowing that almost certainly they would never meet again, and like the Irish way of death, their leaving for a new life was celebrated with drinks, singing, dancing. Set at a crossroads, it passes from night to dawn, with the company moving slowly at first, like the walking dead, and culminated in two sweethearts departing for the New World. 'Lift the Wings', Bill Whelan's greatest song in *Riverdance: The Show*, performed as a duet by ANÚNA's Katie McMahon and Tom McGlynn, underlined the sombre mood of piece, yet it avoided mawkish sentimentality. As expected, 'American Wake' touched a melancholy

chord in the native folk memory and brought lumps to the throats of many of the children's children of those Irish forced to leave their homeland generations before. At the end of the performance there were standing ovations and flowers were flung onto the stage. And the press reviews confirmed that local critics were in danger of running out of superlatives.

Ireland was enjoying another unnatural phenomenon that summer: perfect weather. The sun shone throughout August and the country basked in its second summer of peace. *Riverdance* was the only show in town for newspapers denied their dramatic

staple of politics and courts, and the gossip columnists treated its principal dancers as international stars. There were pictures of *Riverdance* people doing mundane chores, with every utterance of the principals reported in large type. Some stories homed in on Michael Flatley's personal life and his excursions to fashionable nightclubs; others told of his irritation with co-star Jean Butler. Flatley was said to be unhappy. Still, tittle-tattle didn't affect the box office and every seat was sold for the show's six-week run at the Point.

Although it was breaking box-office records and everyone was delighted with its progress, John McColgan, Moya Doherty and Bill Whelan thought they should take the opportunity to introduce changes in the show, to allow it to evolve. They decided to make radical changes for the second London run. The first act required minor adjustments, but the second needed a total overhaul. There had been no time to do any running repairs during the first three short runs but the production team and the promoters were confident that they would be playing London for at least four months. There was one month to work on the changes. David Hayes, always a gifted musician, also showed a natural talent for theatre and was officially appointed Musical Director at the same time as he was given the responsibilities of Assistant Stage Manager. The tap-dancing trio headed home and James Bignon

and the Deliverance Ensemble were going back to Atlanta, Georgia.

A new tune by Bill Whelan, 'Shivna', set to the words of an old Irish verse dating back to around 1175, was added. 'Shelter Me', another new Bill Whelan song, sung by Anna Ross, was the composer's homage to Africa's priceless gift to America, jazz and blues. It was followed by 'Freedom', in which the entire company joined in Whelan's brand-new anthem celebrating the multicultural diversity of the New World. But John McColgan's concept for 'Trading Taps' was a real winner. Two exciting young dancers, Tarik Winston and Nick Holmes, joined the company to beef up the New World sequences and it was obvious from the first rehearsal that they were show-stoppers. 'Trading Taps' featured another world champion, Colin Dunne, who later became the principal male dancer, pitting his virtuoso steps against the astonishing tap-dancing skills of Tarik Winston. Bill Whelan came up with a fascinating blend of American swing and Irish music that flirted effortlessly between the two traditions, integrating the intricate dance steps of both cultures, seamlessly.

Choreographed by Dunne and Winston themselves, it was a competition between two world-class dancers tapping their way across the stage, each urging the other to faster and more daring routines,

Labatt's Apollo, Hammersmith, London.

and culminating in Tarik Winston's pastiche of James Cagney's routine in *Yankee Doodle Dandy*. But where Cagney just ran up the wall at the side of the stage, Winston ran up the wall and somersaulted back onto the stage.

Just after the Moscow Folk Ballet Company's *tour de force*, 'The Russian Dervish', came another new item, 'Oscail an Doras', set in an imaginary Hell's Kitchen in New York where the carefree dancing at the houley is an imaginative counterpoint to ANÚNA's intricate choral rhythms. Unaccompanied vocalising is a Celtic version of scat singing, practised by labourers to relieve the tedium of working in the fields. Although the text of Theo Dorgan's prose poem which linked the sequences was projected on to the stage, the rich, mellifluous voice of one of Ireland's finest actors, John Kavanagh, was recorded and amplified in the theatre to link up the sequences and give a sense of continuity. The revamped show reinvigorated the cast, and advance ticket sales reflected the rekindled interest of the public and the media.

Months later, nearly everyone involved said that they sensed a subtle change of mood both on and off stage, but ignored it. Michael Flatley was unhappy but he didn't, or couldn't, say what was wrong. The British media was particularly taken with

Jean Butler, her photograph frequently appearing in newspapers and magazines. Moya Doherty and John McColgan advised Flatley to hire his own publicist to concentrate on enhancing his profile. An American lawyer had negotiated his contract for the first Dublin run of the show, but Flatley hadn't renewed it. His agreement guaranteed a percentage of the box-office receipts as choreographer plus royalties from the hugely successful video, on top of his salary. It made him a millionaire.

For the upcoming London run, Executive Manager, Julian Erskine, dealt with Flatley's new London-based agent, Deke Arlon. With just two weeks to go before the London reopening, McColgan and Doherty pressed Erskine to conclude the deal. 'Julian told me we have a cast of ninety-one and 85 per cent of his time negotiating was with Michael, and the other ninety members got 15 per cent of his time,' says Moya Doherty. 'I remember Julian coming back to us and saying, "The deal's done", and we went into a pub beside our office in Dublin and ordered a bottle of champagne.' Michael Flatley did return the contract, but he had added ten amendments. Doherty was adamant: 'Nobody is dancing in the show without a contract.'

As the London reopening loomed ever closer, Maurice Cassidy threw up his hands in

frustration and asked Michael Flatley to write down a list of his demands. When it arrived by fax, it confirmed their worst fears: Michael wanted to take over the show. The list was the first concrete proof of how Flatley saw his role. Under the sub-heading 'Changes in the Show', he wrote, 'I would like to include a clause that the producer/directors may not be allowed to make any changes in the show without my consent, at least when I am in the show. I realise this sounds severe but I am genuinely concerned about the people making the creative decisions at present and how it has and will have an effect on the future of the show, especially in America.' While his comments were hurtful, it was another passage that caused alarm. Headed 'Creative Control', it said: 'I would like complete control over all that I do and all that I am involved with in this show. This includes what I wear, when I dance, and which dancers I choose to dance with.'

Barry Clayman offered to mediate and five nights before the show opened, he believed he had finally reached a final settlement with Flatley at 3 a.m., only to be called at 6 a.m. by his agent and told that Flatley would be appearing on a breakfast television programme - he did, and said they still didn't have a deal. Flatley seemed happy negotiating through television: he appeared on one programme and said,

'No, it's nothing to do with money.' And later told the same interviewer, 'I just wanted control over the work that I created myself, that's all.' More ominously, he told the interviewer he doubted if anyone could replace him in the show. There were faxes and phone calls between lawyers, agents and producers. Less than forty-eight hours before the opening, a decision had to be made at a meeting in the west London offices of Jennie Halsall, the show's publicist. It was blindingly obvious to Moya Doherty, who had been very protective of him, that Michael Flatley wanted to have control of the show. Moya Doherty had been very close to Flatley: they were both born within months of each other in 1958, he in Chicago, she in Enniskillen, County Fermanagh. They had come through so much together. It was, she says, 'The most difficult, distressing day of my life and one of the saddest, but the decision had to be taken.' John McColgan, who had always championed Michael's Flatley's enormous talent, felt deeply disappointed. Bill Whelan admired his talent but had had serious professional difficulties with him for months before. Indeed earlier that summer he had received an intriguing letter from fellow composer Andrew Lloyd Webber, telling him that the show was the star rather than any individual performer. Promoter Barry Clayman said: 'We can't go on like this or we will

all be working for Michael. He will take over the show.' Moya Doherty agreed: 'We have to draw a line in the sand; we can't go on like this, we must protect ourselves and the show.' No one dissented when the decision was made to replace Michael Flatley.

It was manic, but there was no panic. At 27, Colin Dunne was ten years younger than the man he was replacing and only heard he was to take the starring role twenty-one hours before the curtain rose. An accountant from Birmingham and winner of nine world dancing titles, he has an arguably better technique as a traditional Irish dancer, but the box office had taken nearly £5 million in advance bookings with Michael Flatley's name at top of the

bill. The media flocked to the theatre in the early afternoon and Colin Dunne appeared for a photo call. Although news of Michael Flatley's non-appearance had been reported all day, Moya Doherty felt queasy when she saw a queue at the box office: was it people looking for their money back? No, they were buying tickets and sales continued to be healthy, with only some forty people asking for a refund over the next few weeks. Then Barry Clayman saw Jean Butler on crutches backstage and told her it was a joke in poor taste. She burst out crying, although it wasn't from the pain of having torn her calf muscles in rehearsals – it was because she would have to watch her stand-in, Areleen Ni Bhaoill, from the stalls when she should

have been leading the company on stage. The audience groaned in disappointment when it was announced that Jean Butler could not perform because of injury; no mention was made of Flatley's non-appearance. 'If you do *Phantom of the Opera* with Michael Crawford and you run it without him, you don't advertise it as *Phantom of the Opera* not starring Michael Crawford,' Julian Erskine told reporters.

The backstage tension primed the dancers' adrenaline pumps and they leapt out of their shoes. Colin Dunne rose to the occasion and the cast urged him to dance faster and higher while they closed ranks and marshalled each routine even more precisely. The *Riverdance* orchestra, with their long experience of the trials of show business, knew the novices on stage needed inspiration and drove them to greater efforts when they weren't nursing them through the more reflective passages. A crisis recognises no

The Riverdance Irish Dance Troupe.

language barriers and the international artists also excelled themselves. As the first act closed, the audience rose from their seats and gave the cast a standing ovation. The revamped second half ran like clockwork. Tarik Winston fulfilled his promise and the London audience were on their feet even before the finale, whistling, stamping and cheering for more. There were hugs and tears in the dressing rooms and emotions were still raw and vulnerable later at the opening party in a nearby nightclub. Like the survivors of a natural disaster, they shared a camaraderie only those who had come though that opening night in the Apollo will ever really understand. The show had come of age, and the combat veterans joked about the two *Riverdance* eras: BF and AF - Before Flatley and After Flatley. Confident the show would run in London for at least four months, promoter Barry Clayman was particularly relieved when Michael Flatley's departure didn't affect ticket sales. 'To have a long-running show, people need to go more than once for it to be successful. There are people who have been to see *Phantom of the Opera* ten times and *Riverdance* is one of these shows.' It broke the box-office records at the Apollo, running for 151 shows, before they all left to take on their biggest challenge yet: America.

Although they had seen photographs and heard the legends, nothing could have prepared the ninety-one members of the cast for Radio City Music Hall. Looking like some vast Art Deco cathedral dipped in gold and preserved in neon-lit aspic, the theatre has a deserved reputation for accurately reflecting the talent on its enormous stage. The most prestigious theatre in the United States cannot be duped by public relations hyperbole. Although they had been prepared for every eventuality, no one thought the stage would be a problem for the dancers. After all, the world famous in-house chorus line, the Rockettes, have high-kicked there for decades with no apparent difficulties. But Irish traditional dancers need a sprung floor to absorb the shocks to the spine and legs from all their leaps and hard-shoe routines. They would have added a more flexible surface to the existing stage, but there was no time: the show was opening in three days. As a contingency, the rehearsal room was transformed into a kind of field hospital, with screens and rows of beds, and a doctor and a team of physiotherapists standing by to massage cramped muscles and deal with injuries.

A promotional slot on 'Late Night' with David Letterman, one of the most popular American network shows, on the Friday before the Tuesday opening, was a resounding success. Closing the show

73 | THE STORY

on St Patrick's Day gave it an ethnic topicality for the media, and its reputation had crossed the Atlantic before the cast: the only problem was fulfilling unrealistic expectations. On opening night, stretch limousines lined up outside the theatre on 6th Avenue, depositing an astonishing gathering of celebrities from show business, industry, banking, brokering, retailing and politics, both Irish and American, for more than an hour before the curtain rose. Senator Ted Kennedy, who had block-booked 60 seats, was joined by his sister, the United States ambassador to Ireland, Jean Kennedy Smith. It was a black tie, haute couture and Tiffany-jewelled evening - with the occasional premature sprig of shamrock saluting New York's Irish week.

There was just one small adjustment from the London production: 'Shelter Me' was replaced with another Bill Whelan song, 'Heal Their Hearts', sung by native New York bass baritone, Ivan Thomas. The 5,854 people in the auditorium didn't quite know what to expect: would *Riverdance: The Show* be another cute showcase for traditional Irish music and dancing, turning Radio City Music Hall into a surrogate village hall? Or a Las Vegas version of an Irish variety show? Most of the audience were standing before the end of the first act; the entire theatre was on its feet for an extended

standing ovation at the close of the show. Producer Moya Doherty was ecstatic: 'You know we're not training the audiences to stand at the end. But there seems to be something about this show that makes audiences in Dublin, London and now New York all stand up spontaneously at the same parts of the show.'

Hundreds of audience members walked the ten blocks from the theatre to the post-show party at the Grand Ballroom of the Plaza hotel - it was like an alternative St Patrick's Day parade. Inside, it was a commonwealth of inherited experience. Corporate lions sat down with cultural lambs sharing a fusion of the feel-good factor and an ethnic bonding that eliminates the social borders separating the barman and the banker, the musician and the merchant prince. With all the champagne that flowed far into the early hours, and all the backslapping, perhaps it just seemed that way. There was criticism, too, from a few first-

ABOVE: *Jean Butler.*

LEFT: *Breandán de Gallái.*

generation Irish Americans, who preferred the native Irish at play as their parents remembered them: maybe a Celtic version of the noble savage, a simple yet happy people dancing at a crossroads to a fiddle and accordion. On stage, the young Irish were slick, confident and, yes, sensual and sexual. It must have been a shock, a bit like seeing a teenage daughter wearing make-up for the first time. Anyway, it was no small feat for a tiny nation on the outer fringes of the north Atlantic, and *Riverdance: The Show* had made it in New York. And if it made it there, they can take it anywhere...

More than a generation of civil strife has sundered the people of Northern Ireland, and the tug of loyalties between the Irish and British traditions is at the heart of the conflict. So in theory, bringing *Riverdance: The Show*, a celebration of traditional Irish culture, to Belfast less than six weeks after the IRA had called off its cease-fire, might have appeared brave, or foolish, or even provocative. The show opened in the King's Hall, a vast multi-purpose exhibition hall more famous for its annual agricultural show, eleven days after it closed in New York. Director John McColgan didn't make any changes in the running order, reasoning that Belfast deserved the best they could offer. It was another black tie and evening dress gala first night, a gathering of the city's business and

political leaders, plus some 3,000 of those brave-hearted citizens who refused to let their community succumb to despair through its darkest days. It was another triumph, and the cast received five curtain calls on the first night, and, according to the *Belfast Telegraph*, they averaged five standing ovations for each of their twenty-eight performances. Rather than highlighting divisions, *Riverdance: The Show* proved to be a force for reconciliation, selling all 3,500 seats for each show through its four-week run.

Taking the show to Millstreet, County Cork, was bringing it back to its roots, and every seat was sold long before the opening. There were people who had never been in a theatre before sitting beside others who hadn't been for decades, and the people of Ireland's southern province, Munster, stood up and cheered at the same parts of the show as the audiences in London, New York, Dublin and Belfast had done. It amused some of the cast that the Green Glens Arena, an internationally renowned show-jumping venue, where they were staging their record-breaking two-week run, had been host to the Eurovision Song Contest in 1993.

Then it was back to London and another season at the Labatt Apollo, where box-office sales had topped £5 million when the show opened on 17 May 1996, for a twelve-week run. Then on to Edinburgh

and a Urals-to-the-Atlantic European tour. In October, the show reopened in Radio City Music Hall in New York, before moving on to Chicago, Los Angeles, Boston and Canada, and then embarking on a sixty-city tour through the United States. The box office in Sydney opened in August 1996 for the show's Australian debut on St Patrick's Day, 1997.

In just two years this heady mix of Celtic chutzpah and cultural glitz had become one of the most successful and innovative theatrical ventures on the stages of three continents. And its international recognition gave Ireland something of a cultural grand slam, coming in the same year that Irish poet Seamus Heaney won the Nobel Prize for literature. *Riverdance: The Show* is now part of an Irish cultural commonwealth, blunting the hard edges dividing high art and vulgar entertainment, where the nation's artists are now sharing their inheritance with the rest of the world.

ABOVE: *The finale, Dublin.*

FOLLOWING SPREAD: *Ivan Thomas and the Riverdance Company.*

 CHAPTER 3

THEMES

RIVERDANCE: THEMES

Before it opened, some academics suspicious of popular taste found it difficult to accept *Riverdance: The Show* as a serious cultural work. And when it did earn aesthetic approval, scholarly interpretations of its storyline sounded rather grand for what is essentially an enormously entertaining two-hour celebration of traditional music and dance. But intellectual snobs and ethnic puritans agonising over the show and its message did perform one useful function: they proved that just because *Riverdance: The Show* is an enjoyable entertainment, this did not mean it cannot also be a serious work of cultural integrity. An earnest Hollywood producer might describe it as 'the story of the journey Irish people have taken over millenniums, an allegory for the history of Ireland and its people from the dawn of civilisation to the present time', which does make the show seem like a vast canvas with weighty resonances, certainly an unlikely vehicle for a box office success. Yet this didn't seem to bother the public

who simply bought tickets, suspended their scepticism, engaged their imaginations and enjoyed the spectacle on stage.

Act One of *Riverdance: The Show* explores the internal journey of the ancient Irish people, first coming to terms with the elements; harnessing fire, water, wood and stone and cultivating the earth; then learning to deal with their spirituality and human relationships, the accumulation of these experiences culminating in their bond with home. Act Two is the outward journey, an experience of many peoples driven from their home by war, famine or slavery to find their way in the New World; and the merging of diverse cultures in a shared adventure which is then transported back home, completing the circle as Ireland celebrates taking its place in the world.

When they first discussed building a seven-minute television interval showpiece into a two-hour stage production, Moya Doherty, John McColgan and Bill Whelan were not sure it could be done. 'Our feeling was that people wanted a *Riverdance* show, but it was

Tall and straight My mother taught me, This is how we dance. Tall and straight My father taught me, This is how we dance.

TRADING TAPS – ACT II SCENE IV

PREVIOUS SPREAD: *Areleen Ní Bhaoill in 'The Countess Cathleen'.*

ABOVE: *Thunderstorm.*

not necessarily possible to deliver it as a two hour entertainment,' said director John McColgan. 'My feeling was that once you executed the body of work done by the Irish dancers, they couldn't repeat it again for twenty minutes and it could only be done three or four times in the show. So you could have seven or eight minutes of that kind of dancing and we didn't believe it would sustain a two-hour show. It just wasn't enough to put up a fiddle player and a girl wandering around singing Irish songs.' Bill Whelan began writing the show in October 1994, less than four months before it opened. 'There is no storyline in the conventional sense of a narrative,' says Whelan. 'In Act One, the show deals with the themes that are at the heart of a lot of the early music and dance, songs in praise of the earth, sun, fire, the moon and other elemental forces that are common to all cultures. Act One is more purely Celtic in form and content. Act Two tells how the native culture has been forced to emigrate and, by so doing, is exposed to the forms of expression of other cultures, both in dance and music. Finally there is a homecoming where the influences picked up abroad are integrated.' John McColgan believed the show would work if they could get other ethnic dancers to excite a neutral audience in the way that Irish traditional dancers did with *Riverdance* in the Eurovision Song Contest. 'I believed that if we could

get people from a deep-rooted tradition, whether it was Spanish, African, American or Russian, and they were excellent dancers, it would work. If they could say something through their dance about their tradition on a subliminal level, it would get through to an audience. There is a shared experience in all cultures, a common suffering of oppressed nations, and audiences tap into truth.'

The show opens with 'Reel Around The Sun', a dance that starts with a slow air and develops into an energetic reel with the dancers' praising the power of the sun. It is followed by 'The Heart's Cry', a haunting song which tells that since the dawning of time love has been the key to life. The 'Women of Ireland' sequence begins with a slip jig, 'The Countess Cathleen', reflecting Yeats's metaphor for maturing Irish womanhood, and it is followed by 'Women of Sidhe' (The Fairy Women), where the women's sexuality is shown challenging the men's. The lament for Cuchulainn, Ireland's most enduring mythological figure, will perhaps prove to be Whelan's most enduring instrumental piece in the programme, and piper Davy Spillane has made 'Caoineadh Chu Chulainn' a regular show-stopper. 'Thunderstorm', featuring the male troupe unaccompanied in a hard shoe dance, is one of the most dramatic and energetic numbers in the programme. A twelfth century verse

was set to 'Shivna', the tale of a seventeenth century chieftain who challenged a saint and was cursed to spend his life in the oak and yew tree forests that covered Ireland at that time. The dreamy 'Firedance' highlights the fatal attraction of this most useful yet dangerous element, and it comes just before 'Slip into Spring - The Harvest', a piece for violin and orchestra that begins gently as Spring and swells with energy and passion to celebrate Summer and the gathering of the harvest in Autumn. '*Riverdance*', from which the whole show emerged, opens with 'Cloudsong' where the spirit of the Riverwoman is summoned up by song and called onto land to awaken the earth, symbolised by the hard-shoe routine of 'Earthrise', which leads to

'*Riverdance*' itself where earth and water come together, bringing the first half of the show to a close in a spectacular climax.

The opening of Act Two, 'American Wake', is John McColgan's poignant reminder of mid-nineteenth century Ireland where famine and poverty drove emigrants from their homeland, many of them to America, sundering families and communities. The Irish made merry at an 'American Wake' before they left for the New World - just as they celebrated death - and this poignant irony is reflected in the 'Novia Scotia Set'. 'Lift The Wings', a song that echoes the heartbreak of lovers leaving for a new life, is one of the highlights of the show. A five-piece suite, 'Harbour of the New World', is a blending of the music and dance of different cultures merging in a sense of shared identity in the New World. 'Heal Their Hearts - Freedom' begins with a lone voice and then others join in as the dispossessed immigrants make their way in a new homeland. The young immigrants' growing confidence is reflected in

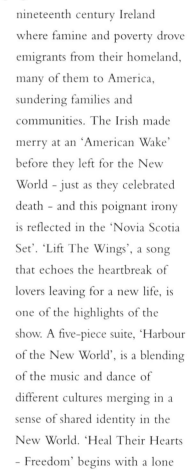

ABOVE: *Maria Pagés*

LEFT: *Freedom*

'Trading Taps' as the young Irish and African American pit their wits and barter their different skills in a dazzling display of contemporary and traditional dance. 'Morning in Macedonia' is a reminder that the New World also welcomed the peoples of eastern Europe, and the 'Russian Dervish' is a thrilling display of acrobatic dancing drawn from Slavic folk traditions. 'Mouth Music', a tradition in Celtic nations and often used to substitute for musical instruments, is featured in 'Oscail An Doras' (Open the Door). It leads into 'Heartbeat of the World – Andalucia', where the torrid rhythms and dance of southern Spain provide a sensual cultural counter-balance. 'Home and Heartland' is the return home for the immigrants who prospered in the New World, their homecoming celebrated with a new-found confidence in music, song and dance. The entire company is on stage for 'Riverdance International', the journey's end when the circle is completed and the island of Ireland assumes its place in the world.

Even Bill Whelan is not that certain about the story – and he isn't sure *Riverdance: The Show* can be described in a one-sentence summary like a film producer's pitch. 'People come out of the show and are not quite sure what they've seen. There's no boy-girl story, no central character. You identify with the music and dance: it's abstract and impressionistic rather than telling a story. We were trying to create a feeling. If people criticise it for not having a story, they are missing the point: it's about feelings and emotions. There is a cultural identification. People recognise something of themselves in the show. How else would African Americans, Australians, people from the north of England identify with the show? Sure, the Irish feel proud to be Irish, but it is international too – and it's not just because of the Spanish or Russian dancers. In Belfast, both Protestants and Catholics identified with it; it transcends nationalism. You have to suspend your preconditioning of what to expect and just let *Riverdance* flow over you. Every generation has to find a new way to express an old idea. *Riverdance* is explaining a people to themselves. It is part of a new confidence for us to express our music and culture in a new way.'

Eurovision performance, R.T.E, The Point, Dublin 1994.

CHAPTER 4

THE MUSIC

RIGHT: *Máirtín O'Connor*

The Riverdance Orchestra.

RIVERDANCE: THE MUSIC

It is one of those chicken-and-egg conundrums: did *Riverdance* make Bill Whelan or did Bill Whelan make *Riverdance*? The glib answer, of course, is that they were made for each other. The show launched Bill Whelan's international career as Ireland's most successful serious contemporary composer, and his music is one of the twin engines that propelled *Riverdance: The Show* from a seven-minute interval in the Eurovision Song Contest to an intercontinental theatrical phenomenon. Whelan wrote all the music and was showered with critical acclaim.

An unusually articulate musician, Whelan still has difficulty explaining *Riverdance: The Show* to those who ask for a precise definition of the story his music is telling. 'You can identify with the music and dance, but it is abstract and impressionistic rather than a direct narrative. We were trying to create a feeling. If people criticise it for not having a story, they are missing the point: it is about emotions and feelings.' But then Moya Doherty wasn't sure if Bill Whelan

would even agree to write the interval piece when she first approached him. 'I thought Bill might not want to be involved with anything to do with the Eurovision programme. We had spoken before that, after he had written the *Seville Suite* and the Mayo piece and was establishing himself as a serious composer. He had made a decision to stop writing advertising jingles and that sort of thing. But we met and I explained what I had in mind for Eurovision and he was very interested. He said, "Okay, I need to find out what Michael Flatley and Jean Butler's repertoire is: if I am writing it, they need to be able to dance it." The minute I heard Bill's draft sketch of the music, I knew it would go brilliantly. It just went right from the beginning.'

Whelan took to the task with great enthusiasm. 'Moya's brief was to write something which would involve dance. It was unquestionably her idea to involve a large group of hard-shoe Irish dancers. I had been working with ANÚNA for a few years and wanted very much to have them on board. Like ANÚNA, the drummers had also appeared in the *Spirit of Mayo*, and coincidentally, it was at the first performance of this

Riverdance

work that Moya saw Michael Flatley and Jean Butler perform. So *Riverdance* did not spring out of nowhere, but involved a continuation of a number of ideas and marriages that had been germinating for some time.'

Marrying music and dance was a specialist skill, but Whelan was confident it would all come together. 'Michael and Jean responded well: he did his choreography; she did hers. Belinda Murphy, the dance captain, worked with the choreographer, Mavis Ascott. Michael did the steps; Mavis did the staging. The first time I saw the line of dancers at rehearsals, I knew it was special, and very, very good. When the rehearsals moved to the Point, there was real excitement. Then the preview audiences, a couple of days before the Eurovision programme, were on their feet. I knew it was going to be strong.' The seven-minute interval eclipsed the other two hours, fifty-three minutes of the 1994 Eurovision Song Contest, but when the prospect arose of extending this interval piece to a two-hour show, Whelan was among the most enthusiastic.

The seven-minute *Riverdance* piece had its origins in Whelan's earlier work. There was his first orchestral work written in 1987 to celebrate the work of Ireland's greatest contemporary exponent of the country's musical tradition, Sean O'Riada. He was composer to the W.B. Yeats Festival at the Abbey

LEFT: *Eileen Ivers.*
RIGHT: *The Riverdance Orchestra.*

Theatre, another invaluable experience. In an interview with the magazine *Dirty Linen*, Whelan said: 'My connection to the works of William Butler Yeats and to the directorial style of the festival director, James Flannery, was enormously influential on my theatrical writing style, to say nothing of its effect in freeing up certain hesitancies I had felt about my own writing. Flannery was very important in reopening my connection to composition.' In 1992, Whelan worked on an album with Andy Irvine, 'East Wind', which explored a marriage of Irish, Bulgarian and

Macedonian music, including time patterns not normally attempted by Irish traditional musicians. Uilleann piper Davy Spillane played on that album with Whelan on keyboards, and Bulgarian multi-instrumentalist Nikola Parov provided the eastern musical mysticism on gadulka, kaval and gaida.

Whelan completed his first large-scale orchestral work, *The Seville Suite (Kinsale to La Coruna)* in 1992. It told the story of the flight to Spain of the forces of Red Hugh O'Donnell after their disastrous

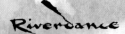

defeat in the Battle of Kinsale in 1601. Commissioned by the Irish government for Ireland's national day at Expo '92 in Seville, the work featured Davy Spillane on Uilleann pipes and low whistle, with accordionist Máirtín O'Connor, members of a Galician group, Milladoriro, and the full RTE orchestra. One of Spain's most celebrated flamenco dancers, Maria Pagés, was featured in the piece. The President of Ireland, Mary Robinson, a native of the county, introduced Whelan's second major work, the *Spirit of Mayo* on stage in Dublin's National Concert Hall in June 1993. It was Whelan's second major work with an 85-piece symphony orchestra as its centrepiece, piper Davy Spillane, violinist Maire Breatnach, soprano Caitriona Walsh and a choir of 200 voices, including Anuna. It was part of the country's celebration of the 5,000 year old Ceide Fields, the field pattern systems and megalithic tombs in north Mayo, the most extensive stone age monument in the world.

But a long time before he stood in front of a symphony orchestra or a 200-piece choir, Bill Whelan was lining himself up for a career in music.

When he was still at school in Limerick in the early 1970s, he wrote the title music for *Bloomfield* (retitled *The Hero* for the US market), a small-budget film starring another Limerick man, Richard Harris. A friendship with Harris led to an introduction to Jimmy Webb, who wrote the actor's inspired and unlikely hit record, 'McArthur's Park'. Whelan was canny enough to complete a law degree before pursuing his musical career, and he worked in orchestra pit bands playing keyboards on the musicals of Andrew Lloyd Webber and Tim Rice. In the late 1970s he joined Planxty, a Irish traditional band with an international reputation,

ABOVE: *Brian O'Brien.*

RIGHT: *Eileen Ivers.*

and played on two of their albums. He had his first contact with the Eurovision Song Contest in 1980, producing the record of 'What's Another Year', which won for Ireland and singer Johnny Logan. The following year, when the Song Contest was transmitted from Ireland, he wrote the interval piece, 'Timedance'. His adaptation of Gilbert and Sullivan's *HMS Pinafore*, which received a Laurence Olivier Award nomination, ran at London's Old Vic before playing in Sydney and Melbourne.

Whelan did most of his television work with director John McColgan, on a wide range of specials and series, and built up a close business and

working relationship which eventually led to *Riverdance*. He did occasional film scores, and was honoured to be asked to arrange and produce an album to celebrate Dublin's millennium in 1988. Along the way, his name turned up on the production and arranging credits for albums by Paul Brady, Van Morrison, Richard Harris, The Dubliners, Hothouse Flowers, Tanita Tikaram and U2. He is very proud of the work he did with leading Irish poets Evan Boland, Nuala Ni Dhomhnaill and Paul Durcan, either collaborating with them or setting their work to music. In 1990 his *Paul Durcan Suite* was first performed by the London Chamber Orchestra. It was

ABOVE: *Katie McMahon.*
RIGHT: *Davy Spillane.*

an impressive bank of experience from which to draw inspiration for *Riverdance: The Show*.

      Besides his talent as a composer, Whelan brought another fundamental element to *Riverdance's* success: the band. He chose the musicians from among his own friends and associates and says they are the best band ever put together for a theatre stage – and the most expensive. And their long experience in show business has been nearly as big an asset to *Riverdance: The Show* as their virtuosity as musicians: willing the company on when it is flagging, and supporting the younger dancers and performers

through crises. The show's first major test was in October 1995, when Colin Dunne stepped in to replace Michael Flatley and Jean Butler was injured, and the producers credit the band's inspired playing for lifting the anxious young dancers' spirits through that crisis and urging them to a higher level of performance than they had ever achieved before.

      Whelan worked closely with Musical Director David Hayes who interpreted his score with great sensitivity. He will be remembered for his great musical landmarks in *Riverdance: The Show*: his 'Caoindeadh Chu Chulainn', a lament for the greatest

figure in Irish mythology, Cuchulainn, played with spine-tingling sensitivity on the Uilleann pipes by Davy Spillane in the first act, will undoubtedly find a life of its own. While 'Lift The Wings', the song which accompanies the parting from Ireland of two young lovers in 'American Wake' in the second act, is a poignant musical underscoring of the tragedy of forced emigration that befell the nation after the famine in the mid-nineteenth century. But Whelan has constantly updated and innovated, adding several new pieces, including 'Shivna', sung by ANÚNA and based on a twelfth century text discovered in the

library of the Royal Dublin Society. His 'Homecoming' piece is a regular show-stopper. But perhaps Whelan's greatest achievement in *Riverdance: The Show* is in bringing sensuality back to Irish music 'The Irish have very often separated sex and spirituality as if they were unable to coexist in one human being. I am strongly of the view that a spirituality without sexuality and sensuality is arid. Sensuality is what much of the work is about.'

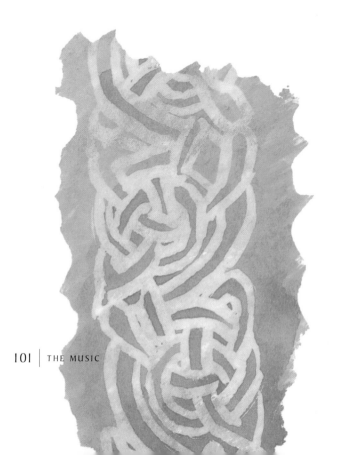

TOP: *ANÚNA.*

ABOVE: *The Deliverance Ensemble.*

 CHAPTER 5

THE
PRODUCTION

RIGHT: *The Deliverance Ensemble.*

RIVERDANCE: THE PRODUCTION

Transferring *Riverdance* from a television set to a stage production needed a leap of imagination and a key figure co-opted on to the creative team: the designer. Although producer Moya Doherty and director John McColgan believed it was a thoroughly modern entertainment, it was vital that the integrity of the concept should be protected – the look of the show would reflect the values of its creators. Yet while aesthetic aspirations were important, there were more practical matters to be considered, such as a simple and uncluttered set. Moya Doherty believed that projection would create the required mood without losing dancing space for the cast. She approached Robert Ballagh, the most famous living painter in Ireland.

As a member of Aosdana, an exclusive association of Irish artists, a fellow of the World Academy of Art and Science and Honorary President of the International Association of Art, Ballagh's credentials were impeccable. His portraits hang on the walls of many public buildings in Ireland and Europe, and in the homes of distinguished public figures and former political leaders. He jokes about his intimate relationship with the Irish people: 'Nearly everybody in Ireland has a piece of my work in their pocket.' Ballagh has designed more than fifty postage stamps for the Irish postal service as well as currency notes for the Irish Central Bank. Although he had designed for the theatre before, an earlier career as a musician in a touring showband had given him an insight into show business.

Ballagh had seen the *Riverdance* interval showpiece in the Eurovision Song Contest and been hugely impressed. 'I thought it touched a nerve in the area of Irish identity in a modern way,' he recalled. The idea of projecting images on a 60-foot wide screen excited him as an artist, and the images he associated with *Riverdance* were inspired by the megalithic passage tombs at Newgrange, Knowth and Dowth in the Boyne Valley in County Meath. 'These extraordinary structures, more ancient than the great Pyramids of Egypt, were built by a mysterious people who were psychically in tune with natural phenomena: all the tombs are aligned directly with the sun and the huge stones used in their construction are decorated with spiral patterns, rich in solar and astral symbolism.' An experienced stage designer, he was used to creating sets which would be built by carpenters and painted by scene

painters, and he pointed out to Moya Doherty that he could make up the projection slides with computer graphics. But while much of *Riverdance: The Show* is state-of-the-art, Moya Doherty insisted on hand painted slides, believing they would complement the integrity of their work. 'An artist makes flat images, and with the projection of massive amounts of light my small paintings would become 60-foot wide,' said Ballagh.

The projection concept was conceived in the can-do optimism of an office long before the practical problems of turning an abstract idea into a reality had to be faced. 'If I had the experience of projection then that I have now, I couldn't be convinced it could be done,' said Ballagh. The first serious complication arose on the night the show opened in Dublin. 'There was a 60-foot wide screen for my projections, wider than you can project with one projector, so we used two. There was supposed to be a "soft focus join" between the two images, but I could see the join and I cringed at the back of the theatre every night,' said Ballagh. And there was a further complication: because each projector needs a second one for dissolves, that meant there were four projectors. These huge projectors used bulbs costing £1,600 each, which needed to be replaced frequently, and there had to be replacement sets of slides ready for when the slides burned out because of the intensity of light projected through them. When the show moved to London, Ballagh simplified matters by designing a 30-foot wide backdrop, the maximum size for one projector, and it was put up in the proscenium arch, with the second projector for the dissolves. Another projector, with a second one for dissolves, was positioned on a balcony facing the stage. The proscenium arch was specially enlarged for *Riverdance* and extended 12 feet into the seating area of the theatre.

When the show returned to the Point in Dublin, and opened at Radio City Music Hall, New York, the bigger auditoria allowed for the dimensions that had originally been planned: a panoramic spread across 80 feet. Ballagh used three screens measuring some 20 feet high by 25 feet wide, and with each

Mavis Ascott and Robert Ballagh.

screen needing two projectors the show travelled with seven projectors, including a spare. And the huge stage at Radio City Music Hall, some 120 feet in length, meant that flats had to be built to fill in the space on either side of the slide screens.

Before the slides can be made, audio-visual specialist Chris Slingsby photographs Robert Ballagh's paintings and artwork, and feeds all the measurements of the set into a computer which calculates where the screen should stand and what the dimensions of the slides should be. The slide makers need this information to ensure that the seven-inch square, custom-made slides for each venue are accurate.

Executive manager Julian Erskine says *Riverdance* is at the cutting edge of projection technology. Because there are no zoom facilities on projectors, precision is essential to ensure that the slide image is in razor-sharp focus. Unlike in the London show, which involved front projection, the images were back-projected in Dublin and at Radio City Music Hall. This caused problems because of the distance required between the screen and the projector, which at stage level takes up dancing space. The manufacturers of the projectors are now developing new lenses for *Riverdance: The Show* which will throw a wider image over a shorter distance without distortion, and allow more dancing space for

> *Cry of an infant*
> *Heartbeat*
> *of the world*
> *Storm against ship*
> *Heartbeat*
> *of the world*
> *Heel against floor*
> *And wave upon shore*
> *Heartbeat*
> *of the world*

HEARTBEAT OF THE WORLD/ANDALUCIA –
ACT II SCENE VIII

the cast. Ironically, it requires an enormous amount of money and a battery of technology to achieve Moya Doherty's original concept of a 'simple, uncluttered look'. According to Julian Erskine, 'The principle always was to let the dancing do all the work and not to complicate it with phenomenal amounts of hydraulics.'

Robert Ballagh says he gets a great thrill from seeing his paintings displayed every night before more than 3,000 people in London and nearly 6,000 in New York. And while he believes the sets are important, they are secondary to the show. 'People don't go to look at the sets, but on the other hand they can complement the show.' The single most important factor in *Riverdance: The Show*, says Ballagh, is 'the energy', although he is still in awe of some of Bill Whelan's music. 'But the more I watch the show and the longer I'm involved with it, I feel it is the kids on stage who bring an innocent exuberance. That is the magic.' A veteran stagehand at Radio City Music Hall summed it up: 'When the guys in *Riverdance* do a

number, the girls hang about to see them and cheer them on. Professionals don't do that.' Ballagh believes a family feeling comes across in the show, and that's what makes it so different. 'It's not a star vehicle. *Riverdance* wouldn't work with six dancers no matter how brilliant they were. What makes it work is the scale of the spectacle. And all this requires a huge investment. But you do get value for money when you go and see it. I've said to the cynics, "If you leave your preconceptions at the door, you will enjoy it." And they generally do.'

Costume designer Jen Kelly worked with Moya Doherty, John McColgan and Robert Ballagh to 'capture the look, spirit and essence of the show'. Kelly said the emphasis was on dance and the fabrics

LEFT: *Maria Pagés.*

RIGHT: *Trading Taps.*

and colours were chosen to complement what he described as 'the *Riverdance* palette'. He designed every costume in the show and says it has changed significantly from the very early days: the original clothing budget was £16,000, whereas the current costumes cost some £80,000. Jen Kelly hopes the girls' costumes look gentle in their Irishness and the boys' costumes rugged. Ironically the Ulster Museum in Belfast picked out one of his Riverdance costumes as 'a contemporary look for the 90s.' Kelly says the most challenging dancer to costume is Maria Pagés whose dresses are made from four different fabrics. 'She dances flamenco in a contemporary style and has

the power to throw 20 metres of cloth around, and she really knows how to play it.'

Some particularly specialist requirements were ordered for *Riverdance: The Show* from sound designer Michael O'Gorman, like the radio microphones inserted in the insteps of the principal dancers' shoes. The microphones are glued on to a tie clip and a cable is run up the dancer's leg and connected to a radio transmitter fitted around their waist. For Maria Pages, the cable runs up the seam of her stockings. 'Everyone wants to hear the loud taps.' said O'Gorman, 'and one of the most important routines is "Trading Taps" where the Irish guys trade taps with the Americans.' O'Gorman says a natural sound works best with traditional music, that it needs to sound as if the musicians are playing right in front of you without amplification, unlike a rock concert where the reverb is part of the occasion. But *Riverdance: The Show* has a very wide stage, and for each member of the audience to get an optimum quality of sound a complicated system of speakers is used to spread the sound around the theatre. O'Gorman has worked for the Chieftains and many of the top rock bands, but he also designed the in-house sound for the 1993, 1994 and 1995 Eurovision Song Contests transmitted from Ireland.

On the road, the production uses eight 45-

Installing Riverdance at Green Glens Arena, County Cork.

foot articulated tractor trailers to haul the set and equipment, and two full-size coaches and a limousine to ferry the cast and crew. They need two large changing room for the orchestra and three, large enough to accommodate twelve people, for the chorus; plus two for the choir, five general dressing rooms and four star dressing rooms. A physiotherapy treatment room is another requirement, as well as a 'Green Room', or recreation area, with tea and coffee making equipment, a refrigerator and a television set with lounge chairs and soft furnishings. *Riverdance*, says Julian Erskine, is the biggest touring show in either Europe or the United States.

ABOVE: *Riverdance, Labatt's Apollo, Hammersmith.*

RIGHT: *Riverdance, Green Glens Arena, County Cork.*

CHAPTER 6

THE FUTURE

RIVERDANCE: THE FUTURE

In the early summer of 1996, Moya Doherty and John McColgan organised a week-long workshop in London to prepare for the future. A year earlier they knew another production would have to be built to satisfy increasing demands from around the world. With the show already committed in Britain and Europe, another team would have to travel to the United States and Australia. Their deadline was October 1996, when one company played London, then moved to Edinburgh and Bournemouth before taking the show to the mainland of Europe, and the second production played in New York, Chicago, Los Angeles and Boston, then for three months in Australia, before returning for a tour of sixty theatres across the United States. The workshop was an ideal opportunity to reconstruct the production and train new backstage staff, as well as to contract new dancers and performers.

Rather than try to create an entirely new show, Moya Doherty and John McColgan decided to use half of the existing cast in London as the base for the second production heading to the United States. 'It suited many of the cast, too. Some wanted to stay close to home, others were keen to travel,' said McColgan. They found a new team of six Russians in

RIGHT: *Susan Ginnety and Colin Dunne.*

Moscow and two flamenco dancers in Spain, then held auditions for tap dancers in New York. And the workshop in London gave them an opportunity to recruit the rarest of talents: traditional Irish dancers. Curiously, as many applicants for the chorus came from the Irish diaspora as from the motherland. Traditional Irish dancers from Britain, Canada, Australia and the United States turned up and competed vigorously with the native Irish for a place on the shortlist of sixty from which thirty-eight would be chosen. The band decided to travel to the United States together and Bill Whelan and musical director David Hayes put together an orchestra in London and Dublin to play at the British and European shows.

Known in the business as cloning, the creation of a theoretically identical twin for *Riverdance: The Show* excited McColgan and Doherty. 'It gave us access to so much new talent. I just couldn't believe there was so much interest in Irish traditional dancing and music around the world. It is a credit to the Irish that they held their cultural heritage so close to them wherever they travelled,' says McColgan. David Hayes, who became Assistant Director at the same time he was appointed Musical Director, took on the challenge of mounting the second Production in eight weeks. 'There had to be two shows of equal quality, there would be no "B-team,"' said David Hayes. 'We split the show and added two new halves to each production. The most difficult problem was to "clone the vibe", the atmosphere is the secret of *Riverdance*.' The new talents thrown up are a major bonus for *Riverdance: The Show* as the pool of gifted dancers and

Maria Pagés and Michael Flatley.

musicians continues to grow, but of course no two theatrical shows with different performers can ever be identical. This metaphysical puzzle would have humoured a compulsive mystic like W. B. Yeats, whose own theatrical ventures involved an innovative and intricate combination of dance, music and drama.

And Yeats influenced both Whelan and McColgan.

TOP LEFT: *Colin Dunne, Bill Whelan, Maria Pagés, Tarik Winston, Eileen Ivers, John McColgan, Eileen Martin.*
TOP RIGHT: *Breandán de Gallaí, Eileen Martin.*

Riverdance

IT'S been a hugely successful Christmas for Irish acts across the water with three of them now riding high in the British charts.

Boyzone climbed all the way to number three before slipping one place to number four — a fantastic achievement for a group formed just seven months ago. Their "Love Me For A Reason" has been a gigantic hit with the band's teenage fans.

☐ JEAN BUTLER

When Ireland won the Eurovision Song Contest for the third year in a row back in 1994, the greatest success story from the occasion was not the winning song "Rock n' Roll Kids" by Charlie McGettigan and Paul Harrington, but the innovative interval act called Riverdance. Since that first standing ovation, Riverdance has been ... into a spectacular show which has taken audiences ... and now New York by storm.

... Choir, Anúna, the fiery flamenco ... — Maria Pages and African ... ers Tarik Winston Jnr. T...

Eurovision — the Donegal connecti...

THE chances are that last weekend's Eurovision Song Contest wouldn't have even taken place without the Donegal connection being involved. For a start, Charlie McGettigan, one half of the winning entry who was brought up in Ballyshannon, w...

would the Eurovision have been without the services of Dungloe-born Executive Producer, Moya Doherty.

If that wasn't enough to lend weight to the theory that the competition ... perhaps be held in ... next year, think ... gaps that would ... in Bill Whelan's ... "without the ... of some of ... finest dancers ...na Bradley, ...muggach in...

Irish dancers poised to sweep us off our feet

Stepping out in t...

What the experts thought of Riverdance

■ BILLIE BARRY, Director of the Billie Barry dance and stage school: "That was the ultimate in dance, tap, ballet and Irish combined into one. People who don't know anything about dancing, and who have no interest in dancing whatsoever were moved by it. Bill Whelan's music was really magic exciting, people are not giving it music enough credit in my ... It's the thing to happen so ... will hopefu... moment, even at Feiseanna McGettigan's taste ... get back into the ... mainstream of Iri... entertain...

coming in, the odd step here and there, the thing about competitions is that you have to make it harder and harder, and now they've set the ... could go, and if you fancy it up, if you fancy ... Irish music has changed, the Iri... thing was bound to happen. Of ... dancing." I say no no, we can ... mber in the days o... you wouldn't eve... nce, now it's mor...

■ CORA CADWELL, Director of the Cora Cadwell Irish dancing school and President of the Comhdháil Múinteoirí Na Rince...

RIVER SHOW

EUGENE MASTERSON

THE spectacular Riverdance from the Eurovision may be about to take the international stage.

A number of impresarios, including Noel Pearson, are believed to be interested in expanding the riveting dance routine into a larger stage show which could tour the world.

British viewers phoned the BBC asking where could they book to see the stage show of Riverdance while continental viewers were also wooed

by Michael Flatley, Jean Butler and their posse of Irish dancers.

A U2-controlled company is also seeking the video rights to the dance routine from the Dublin show which could be marketed all over Europe.

Bill Whelan's tradition... al-based music to Riverd... ance is still topping ... charts here above ... Eurovision winner 'R... 'N' Roll Kids'

River rapture!

Riverdance row ri...

RIVERDANCE The Show will go on — but the fate of star dancer Michael Flatley is not so clearcut.

All that producers of the hit musical, which begins an Autumn run on Tuesday, would say last night was: "Michael has not informed us he is walking away from the show."

A spokesman added that the Chicago-born dancer had confirmed on television on Friday that he would be performing.

Rows

Producers spoke out after reports of rows with Flatley over pay.

Two weeks ago the dancer was reported to have signed a £2.6 million contract which would earn him £50,000 a week but this was denied by producers. Flatley

'NO CONTRACT': Flatley with co-star Jean Butler

Lead star may quit over pay

also allegedly claims he is owed £300,000 and that payment is slow.

Show sources last night said fellow cast member Colin Dunne was being groomed for the lead role in case Flatley pulls out.

Julian Erskine, of producers Tyrone Productions, last week said Flatley's £2.6 million pay claim "was damaging the stability of the show."

He said the show could not afford such an amount and that wages bill.

£50,000 a week would double the

Mr Erskine denied that Flatley

Dance m... on cele...

Integrity

His manager Deke ... "Michael feels his inte... artist is being question... "You don't tell Judi De... to act and you don't tell ... Flatley how to dance."

The show opens at the ... Apollo in Hammersmith, L... this week.

MUSIC HALL NEW YORK

PHOTO CREDITS

Michael Le Poer Trench
4, 5, 20, 21, 22, 41, 42, 48, 54, 72, 74,
81, 86, 88, 94

Chris Hill
16 (top), 24, 28-9, 32, 50, 51, 61, 65,
68-9, 71, 75, 97, 100, 106

Don Sutton Picture Agencies
9

National Library of Ireland
12-13, 15 (top)

Irish Dance Wear, Dublin
15 (bottom)

Mick Hutson
2, 19, 20 (lower), 26-7, 31, 49, 51, 58,
78-9, 96, 98 (top), 101 (top), 107,
111, 116-7

Tom Lawlor
17, 25, 32 (inset), 43, 83, 84-5, 93, 98
(bottom), 99 (left), 112-3

T L Boston
56, 115 (top right)

RTE
36, 91

Stefan Hill
55, 66, 103, 105, 108, 109, 118 (both)

Keith Dobney
37

Robert Doyle
27 (inset)

Colm Henry
6, 7, 38, 40, 46, 47, 52, 53, 101
(bottom)

POETRY

The excerpts from the poetic narrative,
which are featured in the book were
written by *Theo Dorgan*.

IMAGES

Painted images for projection –
Robert Ballagh

Projection software design and
production – *Imagination*

Watercolour illustrations –
Ana Zeferino

While every effort has been made to trace
and acknowledge all copyright holders we
would like to apologise should there have
been any errors or omissions.